Animals I Will Find at the Zoo

RED PANDA

Shannon Anderson

Table of Contents

A Starfish Book

SEAHORSE PUBLISHING

Teaching Tips for Caregivers:

As a caregiver, you can help your child succeed in school by giving them a strong foundation in language and literacy skills and a desire to learn to read.

This book helps children grow by letting them practice reading skills.

Reading for pleasure and interest will help your child to develop reading skills and will give your child the opportunity to practice these skills in meaningful ways.

- Encourage your child to read on her own at home
- Encourage your child to practice reading aloud
- Encourage activities that require reading
- Establish a reading time
- Talk with your child
- Give your child writing materials

Teaching Tips for Teachers:

Research shows that one of the best ways for students to learn a new topic is to read about it.

Before Reading

- Read the "Words to Know" and discuss the meaning of each word.
- Read the back cover to see what the book is about.

During Reading

- When a student gets to a word that is unknown, ask them to look at the rest of the sentence to find clues to help with the meaning of the unknown word.
- Ask the student to write down any pages of the book that were confusing to them.

After Reading

- Discuss the main idea of the book.
- Ask students to give one detail that they learned in the book by showing a text dependent answer from the book.

RED PANDA

A zoo is a fun place to see animals and learn about them.

One animal you may find in a zoo is a red panda.

This animal is called a panda, but it looks more like a raccoon.

Red pandas are not really pandas at all.

Red pandas weigh around 15 pounds (seven kilograms).

Red pandas are also called firefoxes or red bear-cats.

Red pandas live in trees in the mountains.

They have sharp claws that help them climb.

Red pandas mostly live alone.

But moms stay with their babies.

Baby red pandas are called cubs.

Moms have one to four cubs at a time.

Cubs are born with grayish brown fur.

Red pandas are **mammals**, so they feed their babies milk.

Adult red pandas eat lots of **bamboo** leaves.

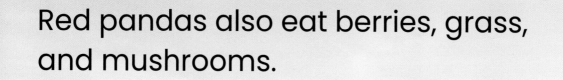

Red pandas also eat berries, grass, and mushrooms.

Sometimes, they eat insects and eggs.

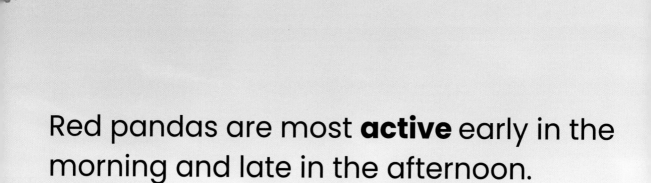

Red pandas are most **active** early in the morning and late in the afternoon.

They sleep in trees during the day.

Red pandas dangle their legs when they are warm and curl up when they are cold.

Red pandas bob their heads and arch their tails to **communicate**.

They also whistle, huff, and quack.

NORTH
AMERICA

EUROPE

ASIA

AFRICA

SOUTH
AMERICA

AUSTRALIA

Red pandas live in **Asia**.

If you cannot go to Asia to see red pandas, you can find them at the zoo!

Words to Know

active (AK-tiv): awake, energetic, and busy

Asia (AY-zhuh): one of Earth's continents; a very large land mass in the eastern hemisphere north of the equator

bamboo (bam-BOO): a tall plant that grows in Asia and that has a hollow, woody stem

communicate (kuh-MYOO-ni-kate): to share information, feelings, or ideas with others

mammals (MAM-uhlz): animals that have hair or fur, that give birth to live babies, and that make milk to feed their babies

Index

Comprehension Questions

1. What are baby red pandas called?
   a. pups   b. kits   c. cubs

2. What do red pandas like to eat?
   a. bamboo   b. cactus   c. lizards

3. Red pandas are from ___.
   a. Asia   b. Africa   c. South America

4. True or False: Red pandas like to live in big groups.

5. True or False: Red pandas sleep in trees.

About the Author

Shannon Anderson is an award-winning children's book author and former elementary school teacher. She loves animals and has eight pets of her own. You can learn more about her or invite her to your school at www.shannonisteaching.com.

Written by: Shannon Anderson
Design by: Under the Oaks Media
Editor: Kim Thompson

Library of Congress PCN Data
Red Panda / Shannon Anderson
Animals I Will Find at the Zoo
ISBN 979-8-8873-5353-1 (hard cover)
ISBN 979-8-8873-5438-5 (paperback)
ISBN 979-8-8873-5523-8 (EPUB)
ISBN 979-8-8873-5608-2 (eBook)
Library of Congress Control Number: 2022949127

Printed in the United States of America.

Photographs/Shutterstock: Paolo Gallo: cover; Edwin Butler: p. 3; Kikijungboy: p. 5; Joanne_Charnwood: p. 6; esdeem: p. 9; slowmotiongli: p. 10; Attila Barsan: p. 13; francesca carmine: p. 15; Adam Brinkman: p. 17; RudiErnst: p. 18; Pyty: p. 20 (map); Ondrej Chratal: p. 20; Saran Jantraurai: p. 21

Seahorse Publishing Company

www.seahorsepub.com

Published in the United States
Seahorse Publishing
PO Box 771325
Coral Springs, FL 33077